OCCASIONAL
PAPER

A Strategic Planning Approach

Defining Alternative Counterterrorism Strategies as an Illustration

Lynn E. Davis, Melanie W. Sisson

RAND
CORPORATION

This Occasional Paper results from the RAND Corporation's continuing program of self-initiated research. Support for such research is provided, in part, by the generosity of RAND's donors and by the fees earned on client-funded research.

Library of Congress Cataloging-in-Publication Data is available for this publication.

The RAND Corporation is a nonprofit research organization providing objective analysis and effective solutions that address the challenges facing the public and private sectors around the world. RAND's publications do not necessarily reflect the opinions of its research clients and sponsors.

RAND® is a registered trademark.

Published 2009 by the RAND Corporation
1776 Main Street, P.O. Box 2138, Santa Monica, CA 90407-2138
1200 South Hayes Street, Arlington, VA 22202-5050
4570 Fifth Avenue, Suite 600, Pittsburgh, PA 15213-2665
RAND URL: http://www.rand.org/
To order RAND documents or to obtain additional information, contact
Distribution Services: Telephone: (310) 451-7002;
Fax: (310) 451-6915; Email: order@rand.org

Preface

This occasional paper defines an approach to strategic planning and then illustrates how one might implement the approach to define alternative counterterrorism strategies, using RAND researchers and research as a resource. It should be of interest to those in the incoming administration as well as throughout the U.S. government interested in doing strategic planning. The paper is also a resource for those involved in defining U.S. counterterrorism strategies inside and outside the U.S. government. This research in the public interest was undertaken by the RAND Corporation using flexible internal research funds.

Contents

Preface iii
Figures vii
Tables ix
Summary xi
Acknowledgments xv
Abbreviations xvii

CHAPTER ONE
Introduction 1
Background 1
Objective 2
Organization of This Document 3

CHAPTER TWO
Defining an Approach to Strategic Planning 5
Current U.S. Approach to Planning 5
An Approach to Strategic Planning 6

CHAPTER THREE
Implementing Our Strategic Planning Approach: Defining Alternative Counterterrorism Strategies 9
Step 1: Define Strategic Goal 9
Step 2: Define Different "Means" to Achieve Strategic Goal 10
Step 3: Define Alternative Counterterrorism Strategies with Means Prioritized 12
    Counterterrorism Strategy 1 14
    Counterterrorism Strategy 2 18
    Counterterrorism Strategy 3 21
Step 4: Facilitate Choice of a Strategy 24
    Choosing Among the Counterterrorism Strategy Approaches 24
    Steps to Take Once a Strategy Approach Is Chosen 25

CHAPTER FOUR
Implementing the Strategic Planning Approach Within the U.S. Government 27

Bibliography 29
RAND Research Used in the Counterterrorism Illustration 29
Other References 31

Figures

S.1. Our Strategic Planning Approach xii
2.1. Conceptual View of Current U.S. Approach to Planning 5
2.2. Conceptual View of Government Strategic Planning Approach 6
2.3. Our Strategic Planning Approach 7

Tables

S.1.   Components of Counterterrorism Strategies xiii
1.1.   Examples of Past Strategic Planning 2
3.1.   Expert Opinions on Which "Means" Should Be Prioritized 13
3.2.   Components of Counterterrorism Strategy 1 14
3.3.   State Department Budget, FY 2009 Budget Request 16
3.4.   Components of Counterterrorism Strategy 2 18
3.5.   State Department Budget, FY 2009 Budget Request 20
3.6.   Components of Counterterrorism Strategy 3 22

Summary

The Need for Strategic Planning

While the U.S. government has historically undertaken strategic reviews and produced numerous strategy documents, these have provided only very general directions for U.S. policymakers. They do not represent what might be called strategic planning: the definition of a strategy in which the means are prioritized to achieve an operationally defined strategic goal.

Many would argue that the setting of priorities is impossible given the complexity of the world. Priorities can also limit the flexibility government departments claim they need to be able to carry out their missions. There is also widespread appreciation of the difficulty of setting priorities within the decentralized U.S. policymaking process. Others, however, do see a need for setting priorities. One reason would be to increase the effectiveness of one's policies in achieving strategic goals. Priorities would also make it possible to allocate limited government resources and provide a compelling foundation for seeking public and congressional support for particular programs. Better efficiencies in government activities could also be achieved by establishing priorities, and priorities could help achieve coherence in the government's overall activities and operations.

The purpose of this study is to define an approach to strategic planning for consideration by the U.S. government and to illustrate its application using the example of the critical national security topic of counterterrorism. To do this, we drew on more than twenty RAND research reports and on numerous RAND experts. It is important to note that this exercise is intended to be purely illustrative: We are not advocating any specific roadmap, operational plan, or bureaucratic solution to the counterterrorism challenges discussed here.

An Approach to Strategic Planning

Our strategic planning approach has four steps as shown in Figure S.1. The approach aims to systematically define alternative strategies and to suggest how one might go about choosing one of the strategies, i.e., the considerations that could lead to the adoption of one strategy rather than another.

Figure S.1
Our Strategic Planning Approach

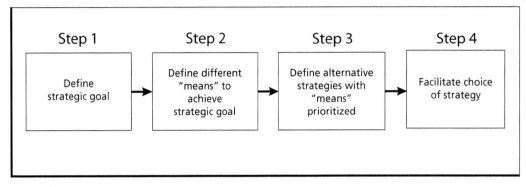

RAND *OP242-S.1*

Illlustrating the Approach: Alternative Counterterrorism Strategies

In our illustrative case, counterterrorism, we defined the strategic goal (Step 1) as:

> **Prevent attacks by al Qaeda and other Salafi-jihadist groups from occurring within the United States that are psychologically significant (i.e., attacks involving tens of casualties or smaller frequent attacks).**

We next defined the full range of available means, or policy tools, making them as specific and distinct as possible (Step 2). We then asked RAND experts for their views on which of the "means" should be given priority and why. These views tended to diverge based on the experts' assessments of the primary requirement for al Qaeda to be able successfully to attack the U.S. homeland.

Based on these varying assessments, we defined three alternative counterterrorism strategy approaches, and then selected the means to carry them out, differentiating those that were "core" priority means and those that could be added, depending on how one views their potential effectiveness in achieving the strategic goal (Step 3). The strategies are summarized in Table S.2.

The final step in our approach to strategic planning is to set the stage for policymakers to choose among the alternative strategy approaches. For counterterrorism, we outlined a number of considerations that could be used to guide this choice. One is whether one of the assessments of what al Qaeda needs to carry out psychologically significant attacks in the United States is correct in its identification of the primary requirement, and if so, the choice of that strategy approach would follow. Another consideration is how well the strategy approaches measure up to what we know about al Qaeda's history of operations and what has worked or not worked in terms of U.S. actions. Yet another consideration is whether al Qaeda currently has, or in the near future will have, the capabilities that match the primary requirement identified in each

Table S.1
Components of Counterterrorism Strategies

Components	Strategy 1	Strategy 2	Strategy 3
Assessment of what al Qaeda needs to be able to inflict psychologically significant attacks in the United States	Maintain active network of individuals and groups with access to resources and communications	Secure territory and establish a base to plan, train, and acquire resources	Motivate leaders and recruits to undertake violent attacks
Overall strategy approach	Disrupt violent jihadist groups' activities through counterterrorism operations	Deny jihadist groups safe havens and resources	Reduce influence of purveyors of jihadist ideas
Core priority means	Assist friendly governments in their ability to operate on their own against violent jihadist groups	Assist states in extending governance, infrastructure, and security throughout their territories	Exploit weakened theological justification for violence; disrupt and capture motivational leaders; encourage defections from jihadist groups
Other possible priority means	Provide U.S. operational assistance; capture or kill highly skilled operational leaders	Seek to deny money, recruits, and conventional weapons to jihadist groups in countries with ungoverned territories	Break up cooperation between al Qaeda and local jihadist groups

strategy. A final consideration is how well the United States could be expected to implement the strategy approach.

If a strategy approach is chosen, then steps would be needed to implement the strategy, including decisions about exactly what the prioritized means will comprise, what programs will be employed, what funds will be allocated, and how the counterterrorism strategy will be integrated with other U.S. national security policies.

Implementing the Strategic Planning Approach Within the U.S. Government

How might our strategic planning approach be implemented within the U.S. government national security policymaking process? In real-world policymaking, the intellectual steps in our strategic planning approach would need to be undertaken in a very different environment from that at RAND: one where officials from many departments and agencies bring expertise as well as strong bureaucratic interests, where decisionmaking responsibility is highly decentralized, and where resistance exists not only to making choices but also to making changes in existing policies.

Implementing our strategic planning approach inside the U.S. government will, therefore, require a top-down decisionmaking process, orchestrated by the Assistant to the President for National Security Affairs, on behalf of the President, and with the personal engagement of the department secretaries and agency heads. The choice of a strategy would be informed by a background paper that would flesh out each of the steps in our strategic planning approach for the chosen national security topic. The key step is defining the alternative strategies. These need to be analytically derived, based on assessments of the factors that might threaten achievement of the strategic goal. The strategies should not be bureaucratically driven and they should not, as is often the case in the government, represent a single bureaucratic-consensus option and a number of "straw man" alternatives.

In the end, even if a single strategy with prioritized means is not chosen, going through the steps in our strategic planning approach has advantages. It can help clarify what one aims to achieve for the specific national security policy topic, uncover underlying assumptions, and illuminate the critical and contentious issues. Most importantly, it would mean a decision to pursue all means without any prioritization was undertaken not by default but, rather, consciously, because it was identified as being the best available course of action.

Acknowledgments

This Occasional Paper benefited from the support and assistance of many RAND researchers. In illustrating our approach to strategic planning, we enlisted counterterrorism experts across RAND and drew on their analyses that spanned the multiple ways the nation is confronting the threat posed by violent jihadists. Our thanks go to each of these experts for their time and insights, and their many analyses that we drew upon are noted in the report. Paul Steinberg was a tremendous resource in helping us organize this paper and in clarifying our thinking and presentation. We want also to thank C. Ryan Henry for his careful and thorough review of our report. We also appreciated the support Dick Neu gave to our effort along the way, offering his insights on the motivations of terrorists and where priorities in our policies need to be focused. Finally, we wish to thank all those who supported the publication of the paper, and especially Steve Kistler, our editor. The content and conclusions of the paper, however, remain solely the responsibility of the authors.

Abbreviations

DoD   Department of Defense

FMF   Foreign Military Financing (U.S. State
                             Department program)

FY   fiscal year

IMET   International Military Education and
                             Training (U.S. State Department program)

MANPADS   man-portable air-defense system

NSC   National Security Council

WMD   weapons of mass destruction

CHAPTER ONE

Introduction

Background

U.S administrations have pursued strategic planning for decades. George Kennan is remembered for launching the nation's Cold War strategic planning when he recommended that "the main element of any United States policy toward the Soviet Union must be that of a long-term, patient but firm and vigilant containment of Russian expansionist tendencies."[1] Presidents from that time on have conducted reviews of policies for the design of strategic nuclear and conventional forces (see Table 1.1).

All of the strategy reviews described in the table followed a similar process: Alternative strategy options were defined, the force structures needed for each were enumerated, and the combination was analyzed with reference both to cost and to the threat the strategies were intended to counter. An examination of these strategy reviews reveals that while the process sometimes resulted in the selection of a strategy, the strategies tended to be comprised of general goals and a list of the multiple ways in which they might be implemented. In other words, although the reviews produced general directions for U.S. policies, and in some cases minor refinements in past policies, none produced a comprehensive strategy that prioritized the key "means" in pursuit of an operationally defined strategic goal.

The administration of George W. Bush conducted a strategic review in the course of developing its 2002 *National Security Strategy of the United States of America*.[2] Since then, the administration has issued a series of strategy documents, including a revised *National Security Strategy of United States of America*, the *National Defense Strategy*, the *National Military Strategy*, and the *National Strategy for Combating Terrorism*.[3] These documents define key strategic goals (e.g., promote effective democracies; defeat global terrorism) and outline steps to achieve these goals. Specific gaps in current capabilities (e.g., special operations forces) are then identified, along with the programs to be undertaken to fill them. Although different in genesis and orientation than the strategic planning reviews in Table 1.1, these strategy documents also provide only very general policy directions; they do not define a strategy based on the use of specific prioritized means to achieve a strategic goal.

---

[1] George F. Kennan (writing as 'X'), "The Sources of Soviet Conduct," *Foreign Affairs*, Vol. 25, No. 4, July 1947, pp. 566–582, reprinted in *American Diplomacy 1900–1950*, Chicago: University of Chicago Press, 1951, p. 113.

[2] The White House, *National Security Strategy of the United States of America*, September 2002.

[3] The White House, *National Security Strategy of the United States of America*, March 2006; U.S. Department of Defense, *National Defense Strategy*, June 2008; Joint Chiefs of Staff, *National Military Strategy of the United States of America*, 2004; and The White House, *National Strategy for Combating Terrorism*, September 2006.

Table 1.1
Examples of Past Strategic Planning

Administration	Name	Description
Truman	Containment	Outlined principles of containing Russian expansionist tendencies but left to circumstances to define political and military responses.
Truman	NSC-68[a]	Called for more rapid buildup of free world political, economic, and military strength, but not implemented because of expense.
Eisenhower	Project Solarium[b]	Chose strategy to maintain enough American military force to help allies build up their forces and to deter further Soviet expansion without initiating a general war.
Nixon	NSSM-3[c]	Formed basis of "nuclear sufficiency" criteria and conventional strategy focused on one-plus contingencies.
Ford	NSSM-246[d]	Established specific goals for strategic nuclear and general-purpose forces requiring major increases.
Carter	PRM-10[e]	Outlined general goals: increase capabilities in Europe; provide flexible forces for Middle East/Persian Gulf; ensure strategic nuclear deterrence/plan limited nuclear options.
Clinton	Bottom-Up Review[f]	Defined areas of force enhancements for major regional conflict, intervention, and peace-enforcement operations.

NOTES:

[a] See President Truman's National Security Council, *NSC-68: United States Objectives and Programs for National Security*, April 14, 1950.

[b] President Eisenhower ordered "a competitive analysis exercise to review the existing American containment policy," called Project Solarium, in 1953. See Tyler Nottberg, "Once and Future Policy Planning: Solarium for Today," Web page, The Eisenhower Institute, undated.

[c] President Nixon's review of the U.S. military posture, National Security Memorandum 3, is described by Robert L. Bovey and James S. Thomason, in *National Security Memorandum 3 (NSSM-3): A Pivotal Initiative in U.S. Defense Policy Development*, Institute for Defense Analyses, September 1998.

[d] President Ford's review of National Defense Policy and Military Posture took place in the fall of 1976. The tasks are described in National Security Council, "National Security Memorandum 246: National Defense Policy and Military Posture," September 2, 1976.

[e] For President Carter's force posture review, see The White House, "Comprehensive Net Assessment and Military Force Posture Review," President Review Memorandum/NSC-10, February 18, 1977.

[f] President Clinton's "Bottom-Up Review" of defense strategy and force structure can be found at Les Aspin, Secretary of Defense, *Report on the BOTTOM_UP REVIEW*, October 1993.

Today's government policymaking and budget processes are not informed by clearly defined strategies in which means are prioritized to achieve operationalized strategic goals. The problem is that it is not possible to make the case for setting priorities in the abstract, and the U.S. government lacks a process to define these in practice. No one in or outside of government has yet designed an approach to strategic planning applicable in the complex and uncertain world that has evolved since the Cold War, when past government strategy reviews were undertaken.

Objective

The goal of this study was to define a new approach to strategic planning and to illustrate how it might be applied, including highlighting the challenges that might be encountered in its implementation.

Applying this approach in a real-world setting in government would necessarily require input from many experts and draw on many resources; however, for the illustration here, we chose to limit the scope of the resources to RAND research and RAND researchers. Because of this, we wanted to focus on a critical national security topic that, in addition to lending itself well to longer-term strategic planning, is an area in which RAND has substantial technical expertise and documented research. RAND has such a body of experts and research on the situations in Iraq and Afghanistan, but the crush of daily operations in those conflicts makes them unlikely candidates for strategic planning. In the end, we chose to apply our new strategic planning approach to counterterrorism. In doing so, we were able to draw on more than twenty RAND research reports and on numerous RAND experts. It is important to note that the application of the approach to counterterrorism in this document is intended to be purely illustrative: We are not advocating any specific roadmap, operational plan, or bureaucratic solution to the counterterrorism challenges discussed here.

Organization of This Document

In Chapter Two, we define the approach to strategic planning that we propose. Chapter Three, which is the core of the report, lays out the application of our approach in terms of defining alternative counterterrorism strategies and of facilitating a choice of strategy. The final chapter describes how our strategic planning approach might be implemented within the U.S. government.

The bibliography details the RAND reports that served as the basis for defining the alternative counterterrorism strategies.

CHAPTER TWO

Defining an Approach to Strategic Planning

Current U.S. Approach to Planning

Figure 2.1 illustrates in broad conceptual terms how national security planning is approached today. As shown here and as discussed in Chapter One, the current approach suffers from a number of limitations. While it does include defining goals and means, they tend to be vague and very general, and there is an unclear relationship between the goals and means and the policymaking and budgeting processes.

As noted earlier, today's government policymaking and budgeting processes are not informed by clearly defined strategies in which "means" are prioritized to achieve operationalized strategic goals. This raises the question of whether setting priorities is either desirable or acceptable. Many would say neither, arguing that setting priorities is impossible given the complexity of the world, the nature of threats, and the lack of policy consensus within the United States and between the United States and its allies. Others would also agree, but for different reasons. Some point to the political risk, pointing out that setting priorities may prove to be politically damaging in the event that things turn out differently than what is projected. Setting priorities also limits the flexibility that government departments and agencies claim to need to be able to carry out their missions. There is also a widespread appreciation of the difficulty of setting priorities within the decentralized U.S. policymaking process.

Others, however, do see a need for setting priorities, for example, to increase the effectiveness of policies in achieving strategic goals. Priorities would also make it possible to better allocate limited government resources, including both the time of senior policymakers and

Figure 2.1.
Conceptual View of Current U.S. Approach to Planning

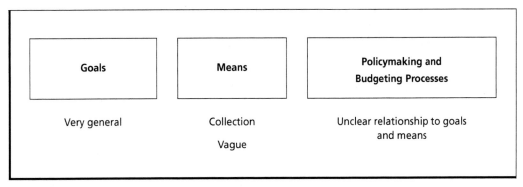

RAND OP242-2.1

actual program funds. Prioritization could also provide a compelling foundation for seeking public and congressional support for particular programs, allowing for clear explanation as to the direct contributions these programs make toward accomplishing a strategic goal. Setting priorities may also lead to increased efficiency in government activities and create greater coherence in the government's overall activities and operations.

An Approach to Strategic Planning

If one wished to do strategic planning within the U.S. government, one way would be to define and operationalize a strategic goal, then to prioritize the means available to achieve that goal, and finally to integrate the priority means into a strategy, which in turn would be used to guide the government's policymaking and budgeting processes (see Figure 2.2).

Building on the approach shown in Figure 2.2, we defined our strategic planning approach with four steps, as shown in Figure 2.3. The first step is to define the strategic goal as specifically as possible. The second step is to define the full range of different "means" one might use to achieve that goal. The third step is to define alternative strategies to achieve the strategic goal, each comprised of a set of prioritized means. Finally, the last step of the approach is to facilitate the choice of a strategy, i.e., the considerations that could lead to the adoption of one strategy rather than another.

Figure 2.2
Conceptual View of Government Strategic Planning Approach

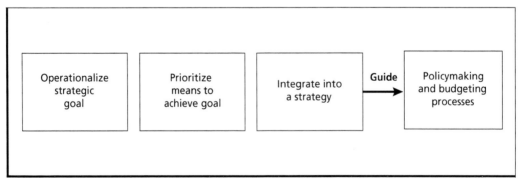

RAND *OP242-2.2*

Figure 2.3
Our Strategic Planning Approach

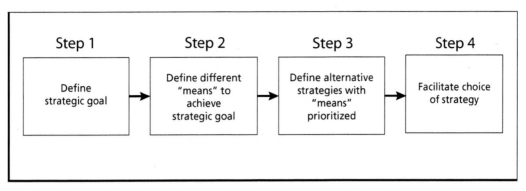

RAND *OP242-2.3*

CHAPTER THREE

Implementing Our Strategic Planning Approach: Defining Alternative Counterterrorism Strategies

To illustrate how the four-step strategic planning approach described in Chapter Two would work in practice, in this section we apply it to the example of the national security policy of counterterrorism.

Step 1: Define Strategic Goal

We sought to define a goal for counterterrorism strategic planning that was both appropriately ambitious and sufficiently realistic. To do this, we first reviewed current U.S. strategy documents that focus on counterterrorism. From these documents, we compiled a list of stated desired ends that ranged from the defeat of global terrorism, to the denial of terrorist access to weapons of mass destruction (WMD), to the prevention of terrorist receipt of sanctuary in rogue states, to the defense of potential targets within the United States.

We then engaged many RAND counterterrorism experts and drew on more than twenty published RAND research reports (see Bibliography) to arrive at a definition of the strategic goal for counterterrorism. A consensus on a strategic goal formed fairly easily:

> **Prevent attacks by al Qaeda and other Salafi-jihadist groups from occurring within the United States that are psychologically significant (i.e., attacks involving tens of casualties or smaller frequent attacks).**

The strategic goal was operationalized in terms of what is being sought (i.e., the prevention of attacks within the United States). Prevention here is understood to pertain not only to the operational phase of an attack but also to attempts to attack—in other words, to precursor activities such as recruiting, training, planning, and material acquisition.

We defined the strategic goal in terms of the threat posed by al Qaeda and other Salafi-jihadist groups based on their overt targeting of the United States in rhetoric and in practice, their broad geopolitical aims, and their material capabilities. While there is debate surrounding some of the specific characteristics of the al Qaeda and Salafi-jihadist threat, there is widespread agreement that it exists and is serious.

The strategic goal was defined narrowly. It does not call for the elimination of these groups or all terrorist violence. Nor does it include specific policies toward Iraq and Afghanistan, even though Salafi-jihadist groups exist in these countries. The complexity and requirements for responding to the situations in these countries call for the design of separate policies.

Preventing terrorists from acquiring WMD and defending the U.S. homeland against terrorist attacks are also related strategic goals, but again call for their own sets of policies.

The scope of the strategic goal was specified as being the prevention of attacks of psychological significance (i.e., attacks that produce tens of domestic casualties or that are of a smaller scale but that occur frequently). We focus on the psychological effects of attack rather than on the scale of attack because even low-casualty events may cause terror and have serious social and political consequences.

Finally, the strategic goal focuses on preventing attacks from occurring within the United States itself. The United States has worldwide interests that have been in the past, and could be again in the future, al Qaeda targets. However, preventing all jihadist terrorist attacks against U.S. interests is not realistic. U.S. efforts to prevent attacks within the United States may, nevertheless, have the ancillary benefit of degrading terrorists' ability to attack overseas U.S. interests. Denying al Qaeda the ability to succeed against the United States could also undermine its ideological appeal and, over time, reduce its power and influence. But the strategic goal identified here is focused on preventing attacks within the United States.

Step 2: Define Different "Means" to Achieve Strategic Goal

The second step in our strategic planning approach is to define the full range of different "means," or policy tools, available to achieve the strategic goal defined in Step 1. Identifying these means was reasonably straightforward. We surveyed current U.S. strategy documents that focus on counterterrorism.[1] RAND studies also provided analyses of various counterterrorism means, with many offering detailed descriptions of activities and funding.

Having collected a list of means, we undertook to define them in some detail, making each as specific as possible and also distinct or functionally independent—none requires the implementation of any other to contribute to achieving the strategic goal. This is not to suggest that there is no relationship among the means. To the contrary, a given means may enhance other means and/or be implemented through the same programs. Rather, it allows for the inclusion of any one means in a given strategy without requiring the inclusion of any other.

The set of fourteen means we arrived at corresponds for the most part to the policies currently being undertaken by the U.S. government. Not included are policies focused generally on democracy-building or promoting the peace process in the Middle East. These policies have important implications for U.S. counterterrorism efforts, but their primary strategic goals differ from the counterterrorism strategic goal identified in Step 1. Policies aimed at reducing the psychological impact of terrorist attacks on American citizens were excluded for the same reason.

In the following bullets, we briefly define what each "means" entails:

- **Means A: Strengthen the indigenous counterterrorism efforts of friendly nations.** To make it possible for friendly nations to disrupt terrorist activities in their own countries,

---

[1]   *The National Security Strategy of the United States of America* (The White House, March 2006) defines essential tasks and then describes "political, economic, diplomatic, and other tools" as well as "steps" to carry out those tasks. *National Strategy for Combating Terrorism* (The White House, September 2006) defines goals to win the war on terror, "four priorities of action," and then for each of these more specific "objectives."

the United States would provide assistance to improve the indigenous law-enforcement and military counterterrorism capabilities of these countries.

- **Means B: Provide operational military assistance to friendly nations in support of their counterterrorism operations.** To enhance the ability of friendly nations to disrupt local terrorist activities, the United States either indirectly (e.g., through advanced surveillance systems) or directly (through special operations forces) would participate in these countries' military counterterrorism operations.

- **Means C: Seek to capture or kill "highly skilled" operational terrorist leaders.** To decrease the capabilities of jihadist groups to mount attacks against the United States, the United States would take unilateral action and/or work with other governments to remove mid-level and top-level operational terrorist leaders through intelligence, policing, and military activities.

- **Means D: Exploit the network technologies used by terrorists.** To decrease the planning and operational effectiveness of jihadist groups, the United States would employ technical assets to compromise terrorists' cell phone or online activity (including chat systems or other multiparty interactions), using these platforms either as intelligence sources or, potentially, to ascertain the location of jihadist leaders or their followers.

- **Means E: Prevent access to specific conventional weapons.** To keep jihadist groups from acquiring advanced conventional weapons such as man-portable air defense systems (MANPADS), the United States and other countries would institute policy, procedural, and technical controls on such conventional weapons as sniper rifles, long-range antitank missiles, and precision indirect-fire weapons.

- **Means F: Deny safe havens to terrorist groups.** To make it difficult for jihadist groups to recruit, plan, train, and acquire resources, the United States would assist friendly governments in extending state control over their territories through improvements in governance, security, public infrastructure, and border control.

- **Means G: Reduce state support for terrorist groups.** To reduce the ability of jihadist groups to operate and spread their messages, the United States would use a combination of political and economic incentives to pressure individual states to curb jihadist activities within their own countries and to prevent the flow of resources from their countries to externally located groups.

- **Means H: Disrupt financial support for terrorist groups.** To disrupt jihadist groups' access to funding, the United States and other countries would take steps to reduce the availability of informal and illegal mechanisms of funds transfers, including implementing regulatory mechanisms to monitor charitable donations and increasing efforts to detect money laundering, black market activity, and drug trade.

- **Means I: Break up relationships and cooperation among violent jihadists.** To limit places where al Qaeda can operate, the United States would employ covert or overt information operations to alter local jihadists' perception that partnering with al Qaeda can help them achieve their own political goals.

- **Means J: Exploit weak theological justifications for violence.** To degrade the ability of jihadist groups to attract leaders and recruits, the United States would partner with respected Islamic scholars and/or local reformists who are authoritative voices within their own societies in order to undermine the credibility of religious and ideological justifications for suicide and the killing of innocents and Muslims.

- **Means K: Disrupt, capture, and prosecute motivational leaders.** To reduce the ability of jihadist groups to recruit and motivate members, the United States would focus on capturing and prosecuting inspirational leaders, who may be more difficult to replace than operational leaders. Locating and apprehending such leaders wherever they might be would require U.S. cooperation with local governments.
- **Means L: Impede recruitment.** To reduce the supply of jihadist recruits, the United States would undertake a variety of information operations to disrupt venues known to be sources of terrorist recruitment. The United States would also work with local governments to monitor and/or close radical mosques and schools.
- **Means M: Encourage defections and facilitate exits from terrorist groups.** To reduce support for jihadist groups, the United States would use overt and covert programs to create financial or other incentives for individuals to defect and renounce violence.
- **Means N: Strengthen the influence of moderate Muslims and their ideology.** To affect the ability of jihadist groups to recruit and motivate members, the United States would seek out a core group of reliable partners among liberal and secular Muslims to counter jihadist ideology.

Step 3: Define Alternative Counterterrorism Strategies with Means Prioritized

The third step in our approach to strategic planning is to define alternative counterterrorism strategies in which some of the previously identified means are given priority.

To accomplish this step, we asked RAND experts to identify those means to which they would give priority based on their view of the contribution each of the individual means would make toward achieving the strategic goal. These evaluations were based on the experts' research on the various means. They also relied on their knowledge both of the more general history of terrorism and of the specific characteristics of recent terrorist operations and attacks. In prioritizing the means, we also asked the experts to factor in the requirements and challenges of implementing them.

As Table 3.1 shows, no clear consensus emerged among the experts. There were many views as to which means should be given priority and on the effectiveness of the individual means.

We asked the experts to explain their choices to understand the sources of the differences in them. Evaluations differed as to the effectiveness of individual means, with the same means in some cases ranked high in priority by one expert and low by another. For example, disrupting terrorists' financial support is viewed by one expert as a high priority because of the criticality of resources to terrorist operations, and by another as a low priority because of how little it costs to carry out attacks. Views also diverged as to how to balance potential gains with the likely political costs of employing some of the means—for example, the civilian casualties likely in attempts to capture or kill highly skilled al Qaeda operational leaders, or the cooperation with nonviolent Islamists that may be necessary in breaking up relationships among violent jihadists.

It was clear, however, that the main reason for the differences in the experts' prioritization of the various means was their differing assessments of al Qaeda's requirements for successfully mounting an attack on the U.S. homeland. Some believe that al Qaeda's primary need is

Table 3.1
Expert Opinions on Which "Means" Should Be Prioritized

Means	Experts													
	1	2	3	4	5	6	7	8	9	10	11	12	13	14
A. Strengthen friendly nations' indigenous counterterrorism efforts	X	X	X	X	X	X	X	X						
B. Provide operational military assistance to friendly nations in support of their counter-terrorism operations	X			X	X	X			X					
C. Capture or kill "highly skilled" operational leaders	X	X					X		X					
D. Exploit network technologies used by terrorists		X									X			
E. Prevent access to specific conventional weapons									X			X		
F. Deny safe havens to terrorist groups					X	X				X	X	X		
G. Reduce state support for terrorist groups											X	X		
H. Disrupt financial support for terrorists											X			
I. Break up relationships and cooperation among violent jihadists	X			X			X							
J. Exploit weak theological justification for violence			X											X
K. Disrupt, capture, and prosecute motivational leaders							X						X	X
L. Impede terrorist recruitment										X		X		
M. Encourage defections and facilitate exits from groups								X					X	X
N. Strengthen influence of moderate Muslims and their ideology to prevail in war of ideas								X		X			X	X

the ability to maintain an active network of leaders and groups that are able to communicate, transfer materials, and operate globally, while others view a secure base at which al Qaeda can recruit and train members and plan and resource attacks as the essential requirement. For still others, the primary requirement is the ability to disseminate a persuasive ideology that motivates leaders and recruits to undertake violent attacks.

Based on these varying assessments of al Qaeda's primary requirement for conducting psychologically significant attacks within the United States, we defined distinct counterterrorism strategy approaches. We then selected the priority means to carry out the strategy approach, differentiating those that were "core" priority means and those that could be added, depending on how one views their potential effectiveness in achieving the strategic goal.

Other counterterrorism strategies could be defined, and indeed, right after 9/11, the Bush administration gave priority to capturing and killing al Qaeda leaders in Afghanistan and ending the support they received from the Taliban government. It was only after the military operations ended in Afghanistan that counterterrorism means proliferated and priorities disappeared. It is important to note that in each of the counterterrorism strategies described below, the prioritization of some means over others does not imply the others would not be pursued at all; prioritization indicates only that certain means are given more emphasis than others when policymakers are allocating time and budget resources. Other means could still be integrated into the strategy, for example, with the aim of enhancing the effectiveness of the prioritized means.

What follows is a description of the three counterterrorism strategies we identified. Each is comprised of four components: (1) an assessment of what al Qaeda and other Salafi-jihadist groups need to carry out psychologically significant attacks within the United States; (2) an overall strategy approach; (3) core priority means; and (4) other possible means, where decisions are required as to whether to also give them priority in the strategy.

Counterterrorism Strategy 1

This strategy (summarized in Table 3.2), is based on the assessment that al Qaeda's primary requirement in being able to carry out psychologically significant attacks within the United States is the ability to maintain an active network of leaders and groups that have access to resources and are able to communicate and operate globally. The overall approach in Strategy 1 is to disrupt the communication, planning, equipping, and operational activities of violent jihadists in friendly countries through intelligence, police, and military counterterrorism operations.[2]

Strategy 1: Core Priority Means. The core priority means in this strategy is for the United States to provide assistance to friendly governments to enable them to operate successfully, *on their own*, against violent jihadist individuals, cells, and groups active within their countries. The goal of these operations would be to keep violent jihadists under unremitting pressure so they are unable to plan or to launch attacks within the United States. Indigenous police and intelligence operations would be employed to intercept and monitor terrorist communications, penetrate terrorist cells, apprehend members, and destroy command structures and sources of logistical support. Paramilitary and military operations, including psychological operations, could also be used, especially where violent jihadist groups are supporting an insurgency against the government.[3]

Table 3.2
Components of Counterterrorism Strategy 1

Component	Counterterrorism Strategy 1
Assessment of what al Qaeda needs to be able to inflict psychologically significant attacks in United States	Maintain active network of individuals and groups with access to resources and communications
Overall approach	Disrupt violent jihadist groups' activities through counterterrorism operations
Core priority means	Assist friendly governments in their ability to operate on their own against violent jihadist groups
Other possible priority means	Provide U.S. operational assistance (?) Capture or kill highly skilled operational leaders (?)

---

[2] Means A.

[3] For RAND research that describes the characteristics of this core priority means, see Seth G. Jones and Martin Libicki, *How Terrorist Groups End: Lessons for Countering al Qa'ida,* Santa Monica, Calif: RAND Corporation, MG-741/1-RC, 2008; Adam Grissom and David Ochmanek, *Train, Equip, Advise, Assist: The USAF and the Indirect Approach to Countering Terrorist Groups Abroad,* Santa Monica, Calif.: RAND Corporation, MG-699-AF, 2008, not available to the general public; David Ochmanek, *Military Operations Against Terrorist Groups Abroad: Implications for the United States Air Force,* Santa Monica, Calif.: RAND Corporation, MR-1738-AF, 2003; Jennifer D. P. Moroney, Nancy E. Blacker, Renee Buhr, James McFadden, Cathryn Quantic Thurston, and Anny Wong, *Building Partner Capabilities for Coalition Operations,* Santa Monica, Calif.: RAND Corporation, MG-635-A, 2007; Jones, Seth G., Jeremy M. Wilson, Andrew Rathmell, and K. Jack Riley, *Establishing Law and Order After Conflict,* Santa Monica, Calif.: RAND Corporation, MG-374-RC, 2005; David C. Gompert, John Gordon, IV, Adam Grissom, David R. Frelinger, Seth G. Jones, Martin C. Libicki, Edward O'Connell, Brooke K. Stearns, and Robert E. Hunter, *War by Other Means: Building Complete and Balanced Capabilities for Counterinsurgency,* Santa Monica, Calif.: RAND Corporation, MG-595/2-OSD, 2008.

The United States would support these civilian counterterrorism operations by providing funding for improvements in law enforcement (including police and paramilitary forces) and intelligence capabilities. Depending on the situation in the individual countries, the United States could also provide military assistance that could range from different levels of military education and training to equipping their forces with military, intelligence, and communications equipment.

Strategy 1 requires the identification of the friendly countries that would be the focus of these assistance programs, a considerable challenge given the nature of al Qaeda today. Al Qaeda's network is broad and global, a combination of a coordinated leadership and autonomous or semiautonomous collections of individuals, cells, and groups. Its activities cross state borders, and, historically, attacks have been planned and carried out by individuals and cells in multiple locations. The bombing of the USS *Cole*, for example, was planned and executed by sixteen members living in three nations; the 9/11 attacks were perpetrated by nineteen suicide attackers with the support of cells operating in five different countries.[4]

Classified intelligence on al Qaeda and other violent jihadist groups may make it possible to map this network (or these networks) in some detail. This map could then be used to produce a list of friendly countries in which nodes of the network are located. These may be areas in which recruitment or training are taking place, where the leadership cadre resides, centers of communication are located, sources from which funding or equipment flow, or the locations to which funding and equipment flow.

Specific countries would then be chosen to receive U.S. assistance based on an assessment of which terrorist activities present the greatest and/or most imminent threat of attack on the United States; these could include countries where high-level leaders are present, where communications hubs appear, or where money, materials, and skilled personnel (e.g., bombmakers) are collecting. Countries where jihadists are operating only with local agendas and, thus, are not linked to al Qaeda's global ambitions, would not be chosen.

With these criteria in mind, and drawing on RAND experts and background studies, the friendly countries that appear to warrant a focus should Strategy 1 be implemented today would be, in addition to U.S. NATO allies (Britain, France, and Turkey), Algeria, Kuwait, Morocco, Pakistan, Saudi Arabia, and Yemen.[5]

Implementation. The United States has a variety of security assistance programs that could be leveraged to implement this strategy. State Department programs include Foreign Military Financing (FMF), which provides military training and equipment, and International Military and Education Training (IMET), which provides professional military education. In addition, since 9/11, the State Department has instituted four counterterrorism programs. The Anti-Terrorism Assistance Program provides U.S. training and assistance to strengthen the counterterrorism capabilities of partner law enforcement agencies. The Counterterrorism Finance Program assists partners in detecting, isolating, and dismantling terrorist financial

---

[4] The Tawfiq bin Attash Network was responsible for the USS *Cole* bombing, with its sixteen members living in Yemen, Saudi Arabia, and the UAE. The Mohammad Atta Network, which was responsible for the 9/11 attacks, had cells located in Germany, Morocco, Malaysia, Afghanistan, and Saudi Arabia. See Kim Cragin and Scott Gerwehr, *Disuading Terror: Strategic Influence and the Struggle Against Terrorism*, Santa Monica, Calif.: RAND Corporation, MG-184-RC, 2005, pp. 41–52.

[5] One RAND study defines countries facing "a prominent military jihadist threat" (Grissom and Ochmanek, 2008, pp. 30–34). Another RAND study focuses on key locations where al Qaeda has a foothold (Jones and Libicki, 2008, p. 132).

networks. The Terrorist Interdiction Program/Personal Identification Secure Comparison and Evaluation System provides computerized watch listing systems to enable immigration and border-control officials to identify suspect persons attempting to enter and leave their countries. The Counterterrorism Engagement Program seeks to build international political will in the war on terrorism and facilitates regional counterterrorism efforts.[6]

The United States today cooperates bilaterally and through multilateral organizations with European countries in a variety of counterterrorism activities. U.S government agencies also support counterterrorism operations in a variety of other countries throughout the world. In 2009, the State Department proposes to provide some form of antiterrorism assistance to over 40 countries.

Table 3.3 displays the State Department's fiscal year (FY) 2009 proposals for counterterrorism assistance and security assistance (FMF and IMET) for the six countries other than U.S. NATO allies defined above as a possible focus for Strategy 1, along with the percentage of the total received together by these six countries. If this strategy were to be implemented, policymakers would be in a position to ensure that these countries were given priority in these program budgets.

The Department of Defense (DoD) has also created programs since 9/11 that focus on building the counterterrorism capabilities of friendly countries. The Combating Terrorism Fellowship Program is distributed through the geographic combatant commanders and provides funding for educating foreign military officers and government security officials in various tactical and strategic operational concepts for combating terrorism. Proposed funding in FY 2009 is $35 million. The DoD also funds Global Train and Equip programs, which are designed to meet time-sensitive and emerging threats and enable the Secretary of Defense, with the concurrence of the Secretary of State, to expedite the training (e.g., in counterterrorism, air assault, maritime interdiction, and border security) and equipping (e.g., with coastal surveillance stations, communications upgrades, small arms weapons, and radios) of friendly governments.

Table 3.3
State Department Budget, FY 2009 Budget Request

	Counterterrorism Assistance Programs	Foreign Military Financing	IMET
Total budget ($ thousands)	145,500	4,812,000	89,100
Algeria ($ thousands)	400	0	800
Kuwait ($ thousands)	0	0	15
Morocco ($ thousands)	425	3,655	1,725
Pakistan ($ thousands)	10,500	300,000	1,950
Saudi Arabia ($ thousands)	0	0	15
Yemen ($ thousands)	1,315	3,000	1,000
Six countries as % of total	9%	6%	18%

SOURCE: Congressional Budget Justification, Foreign Operations, Fiscal Year 2009.

NOTE: Total budget for IMET and Counter-Terrorism Assistance Programs excludes Afghanistan funding. Total budget for FMF excludes funding for Israel and Egypt.

---

[6] U.S. Department of State, *Congressional Budget Justification, Foreign Operations, Fiscal Year 2009*, February 19, 2008, pp. 68, 112, 115, 130.

For FY 2009, the DoD is proposing to fund $500 million for its Global Train and Equip Program, with Pakistan as one of the recipients.[7]

Challenges. The biggest challenge in implementing the core priority means for Strategy 1 involves finding governments willing to conduct counterterrorism operations against violent jihadist individuals and groups within their countries. Another challenge is making available the necessary military assistance resources, given U.S. commitments in Iraq and Afghanistan. Gaining congressional support for the provision of security assistance funds can also be problematic where the recipients are countries with authoritarian governments and poor human rights records.

Strategy 1: Other Possible Priority Means. Having defined the core priority means in Strategy 1, the next step is to decide whether to include as a priority direct U.S. involvement in the overseas counterterrorism operations of friendly countries. [8]

One such means would be for the United States to provide operational military assistance, for example, by providing and operating advanced surveillance and secure communications systems, border and coastal monitoring capabilities, and tactical and theater air-transport planes. An example of intelligence and reconnaissance support would be the supply and operation of unmanned aerial vehicles. The United States could also employ its own military forces directly, for example, by attacking high-value targets in remote or populated areas or by supporting operations from the air or with special operations personnel.[9]

The argument for introducing operational U.S. military assistance as a priority in this strategy is that, without such assistance, it is unlikely that partner countries will be able to keep sufficient pressure on jihadist groups to disrupt their activities (for lack of intelligence capabilities, military skills, or equipment). The argument against a U.S. operational role is that such actions could prove counterproductive, given their potential to produce a backlash from indigenous populations both against the United States and against their own governments. A direct U.S. military role could even have the effect of *increasing* terrorist recruitment.

Another possible additional operational means for Strategy 1 is for the United States to give priority to the capture or killing of highly skilled mid- and high-level al Qaeda operational leaders.[10] This could be done unilaterally or with the cooperation of indigenous governments. Such operations would focus on locating, apprehending, or killing leaders wherever they might be. Although police and law enforcement would be the preferred means, military operations could be required.[11]

The argument in favor of giving priority in Strategy 1 to this means is that these leaders are important to al Qaeda's ability to operate globally and, more important, to be able to carry out attacks within the United States. The argument against giving this means priority is that al Qaeda can replace such leaders and that this type of operation risks producing backlash throughout the Muslim world.

---

[7]   U.S. Department of Defense, Defense Security Cooperation Agency, *Fiscal Year (FY) 2009 Budget Estimates,* February 2008, pp. 419–420, 422–427.

[8]   Means B.

[9]   For RAND research that describes the characteristics of this means, see Grissom and Ochmanek, 2008; and Ochmanek, 2003.

[10]   Means C.

[11]   For RAND research describing the characteristics of this means, see Jones and Libicki, *2008;* Stephen T. Hosmer, *Operations Against Enemy Leaders*, Santa Monica, Calif.: RAND Corporation, MR-1385-AF, 2001; and Ochmanek, 2003.

Counterterrorism Strategy 2

This strategy (summarized in Table 3.4) is based on the assessment that al Qaeda's primary requirement in being able to carry out psychologically significant attacks within the United States is their ability to secure territory in which they can establish a base at which to plan, train, and acquire resources. The overall approach in Strategy 2 is to deny jihadist groups safe havens and access to resources.

Strategy 2: Core Priority Means. The core priority means in this strategy is to assist states in extending governance, infrastructure, and security throughout their territories.[12] The focus would be on enabling governments to extend their institutions and services and to obtain and maintain a monopoly on the use of force. They would seek to eliminate corruption in their law enforcement and border security agencies and to counter the activities of illegal drug cartels and other criminal groups. They would also undertake to provide security (at airports, for public transportation, and in communities); to invest in infrastructure projects, such as expanding road and rail networks; and to provide utilities, health care, and education.[13]

Strategy 2 requires identifying countries with ungoverned territories where jihadist groups currently have a base or where they might seek to establish a base in the future. A recent RAND report, comprised of detailed case studies of countries in multiple regions of the world, undertook to identify these countries by assessing the extent to which they contain territories that are "ungoverned" and "conducive" to a terrorist presence. This research argues that ungovernability exists in a state when any of the following conditions are met: State penetration of society is low; the state does not have a demonstrable monopoly on the use of force; the state cannot control its borders; and/or the state is subject to the external intervention of other states. Conduciveness addresses the environmental factors that facilitate terrorist group operations, such as access to communications infrastructure, banking systems, and transportation networks. The nature and demographics of the surrounding society—the existence of informal social networks, extremist groups, criminal syndicates, supportive norms, and a pre-existing state of violence—also contribute to a territory's conduciveness to terrorist operations.[14]

Table 3.4
Components of Counterterrorism Strategy 2

Component	Counterterrorism Strategy 2
Assessment of what al Qaeda needs to be able to inflict psychologically significant attacks in United States	Secure territory and establish a base to plan, train, and acquire resources
Overall strategy approach	Deny jihadist groups safe havens and resources
Core priority means	Assist states in extending governance, infrastructure, and security throughout their territories
Other possible priority means	Seek to deny money, recruits, and conventional weapons to jihadist groups in countries with ungoverned territories (?)

[12] Means F.

[13] For RAND research describing the characteristics of this core priority means, see Rabasa, Angel, Steven Boraz, Peter Chalk, Kim Cragin, Theodore W. Karasik, Jennifer D. P. Moroney, Kevin A. O'Brien, and John E. Peters, *Ungoverned Territories: Understanding and Reducing Terrorism Risks*, Santa Monica, Calif.: RAND Corporation, MG-561-AF, 2007; and Marla C. Haims, David C. Gompert, Gregory F. Treverton, and Brooke K. Stearns, *Breaking the Failed-State Cycle*, Santa Monica, Calif.: RAND Corporation, OP-204-HLTH/NDRI/A/AF, 2008.

[14] Rabasa et al., 2007, pp. 7–21.

The RAND experts concluded that Pakistan, Nigeria, and the Philippines currently meet the above criteria of ungovernability and conduciveness to terrorist presence. The region of the Pakistan-Afghanistan border exhibits an almost complete lack of state penetration, with lax or nonexistent controls, the absence of a government monopoly on the use of force, and resistance to state authority by local tribes. In terms of conduciveness to terrorist presence, this region is home to a multitude of extremist religious, ethnic, and criminal entities and has a population that maintains values and norms that promote hospitality toward such groups. This region is also where the core al Qaeda leadership is believed to have taken refuge.

Although Nigeria has relatively functional state institutions, it remains subject to extreme levels of corruption and crime; is a conduit for the trafficking of drugs, money, and weapons; and houses a population in which Islamic radicalism is on the rise. Its attractiveness to terrorists is attributable to the presence of sources of income and favorable demographics.

The Philippine island of Mindanao has a legacy of longstanding insurgencies, ineffective institutions, and the presence of armed extremist groups. The government has little control over Mindanao's borders, vast tracts of the island's inhospitable terrain are effectively outside the central authority's purview, and the indigenous population is poor, ethnically and religiously polarized, and resistant to government rule.[15]

At the same time, it is possible that al Qaeda might seek to relocate to other ungoverned areas should Pakistan become inhospitable or as foreign fighters depart Iraq. Strategy 2 would therefore also focus on engaging countries with ungoverned territories that are currently less conducive to terrorist presence, but where jihadists might seek a safe haven in the future. Drawing on RAND studies and experts, we identified Mali, Somalia, and Yemen as such countries.[16]

In the countries selected, the United States would focus on helping the governments to extend their authority, improve border controls, secure a monopoly on the use of force, and provide various development programs.

Implementation. A variety of State Department assistance programs, while not having goals that are directly linked to countering jihadists in ungoverned territories, could be used to implement Strategy 2, including those that fall under Development Assistance; Peace and Security (Stabilization Operations); Governing Justly (Good Governance and Civil Society); Investing in People; and Economic Growth. Table 3.5 lists some of these programs, and also the FY 2009 proposed funding for the six countries chosen to be the focus of Strategy 2. Because the allocations for these programs are undertaken with other goals in mind, it is not surprising that these countries do not rank highly; however, if Strategy 2 were adopted, redistributions could be made. Funds in the State Department International Narcotics and Law Enforcement program also provide assistance to Pakistan for border security, law enforcement, and judicial system reform.[17]

The DoD has also recently established the Security and Stabilization Assistance authority, which allows it to fund the Department of State to send civilians to implement stabilization missions. This is another potential program for supporting Strategy 2. In the past, these funds

---

[15] Rabasa et. al, 2007, pp. 49–76, 111–145, 173–205.

[16] Further evaluation of the ungovernability and conduciveness of additional states could add to this list of countries meriting focus in Strategy 2, although some states may be unlikely candidates for U.S. assistance for political reasons.

[17] U.S. Department of State, 2008, p. 54.

Table 3.5
State Department Budget, FY 2009 Budget Request

	Development Assistance	Stabilization Operations	Good Governance	Civil Society	Investing in People	Economic Growth
Total budget ($ thousands)	1,639,055	5,521,127	533,308	398,033	7,709,726	2,339,173
Mali ($ thousands)	27,485	250	3,000	1,000	32,996	16,000
Nigeria ($ thousands)	37,500	2,150	5,400	3,500	454,522	12,500
Pakistan ($ thousands)	0	323,650	33,200	9,421	259,575	118,859
Philippines ($ thousands)	56,703	18,100	2,997	0	33,117	31,808
Somalia ($ thousands)	0	15,600	4,500	2,000	9,730	0
Yemen ($ thousands)	21,000	5,500	1,500	2,500	16,478	3,000
Six countries as % of total	9%	7%	9%	5%	10%	8%

SOURCE: Congressional Budget Justification, Foreign Operations, Fiscal Year 2009.

have been used in Somalia to help that country improve cross-border security, in Yemen to institutionalize good governance practices through the provision of services, and in the trans-Sahara countries to reduce terrorist sanctuaries and recruiting. The budget request in FY 2009 is $200 million.[18]

Challenges. The first challenge in implementing the core priority means for Strategy 2 is the need for support for such efforts within the countries with ungoverned territories. Equally important is the design and implementation of a multifaceted and long-term development and security effort, which the international community has struggled to accomplish in the past. Such an effort would require resources not only from agencies across the U.S. government but also from other countries, as well as the support of global and regional financial institutions. An effective oversight mechanism will be needed to ensure that assistance funding is not diverted by entrenched corruption in recipient countries. There is also danger that the development of infrastructure will be vulnerable to exploitation by terrorist organizations before the government institutions needed to monitor or interrupt their activities are put in place. If so, this could temporarily increase rather than decrease a territory's appeal as a base.

Strategy 2: Other Possible Priority Means. Having defined the core priority means in Strategy 2, the next step is to decide whether to add as a priority other means that would aim to make ungoverned territories less attractive to jihadists by reducing the availability of different types of resources.

One such means would be to disrupt the sources of financial support for jihadist individuals and groups.[19] For example, the United States could help the governments of countries with ungoverned territories to develop modern banking systems capable of tracking financial transactions and identifying and prosecuting money laundering, reducing the prevalence of criminal activities that fund terrorists, such as drug and arms trading, and suppressing black

---

[18] U.S. Department of Defense, Defense Security Cooperation Agency, 2008, pp. 427–430.

[19] Means H.

and gray economies. More globally, steps could be taken to track and regulate the flow of finances from Islamic charities and nongovernmental organizations into these countries.

Another potential priority means in Strategy 2 would be for the United States to put pressure on states worldwide to curb jihadist activities in their own countries, thereby decreasing the flow of resources from local sympathizers to jihadists in countries with ungoverned territories. This would entail, for example, closing down radical mosques at which jihadists recruit and spread their ideology or regulating financial transactions between local charities and entities abroad. States would be encouraged in such activities via a combination of U.S. political and economic incentives and pressures.[20]

Finally, another potential priority means would be to use national and multilateral regulatory and technical measures to deny jihadists access to advanced conventional weaponry—weaponry developed for ordinary military forces but that if acquired by terrorists might be used in novel or unexpected ways in an attack on the United States.[21] Building on the international community's effort to control MANPADS, the focus of this means would be on the countries with ungoverned territories and those along their borders, with the aim of denying jihadist groups such conventional weapons as sniper rifles and associated instrumentation, long-range antitank missiles, large limpet mines, and precision indirect-fire weapons.[22]

The argument for or against including these three additional means as priorities in Strategy 2 turns on whether simply reducing, as opposed to denying, the flow of resources to these groups in the form of funds, recruits, and conventional weapons can be expected to make any real difference in the ability of jihadist groups to carry out attacks within the United States. And in the case of each of these means, there are obstacles to their successful implementation. For example, states, even if they are supportive, have difficulty preventing the flow of funds and potential recruits out of their countries, given the globalization of finances and the ease of travel across borders. Multilateral agreements can be negotiated to impose controls on the flow of conventional weapons, but such controls will necessarily be voluntary on the part of governments, and to be effective such controls would need support from all countries in which these weapons are manufactured.

Counterterrorism Strategy 3

This strategy (summarized in Table 3.6) is based on the assessment that al Qaeda's primary requirement in being able to carry out psychologically significant attacks within the United States is their ability to motivate operational leaders and recruits to undertake violent attacks. The overall approach in Strategy 3 is to reduce the influence of purveyors of jihadist ideas.

Strategy 3: Core Priority Means. The core priority means in this strategy involves a series of steps taken against those holding and spreading jihadist ideas. First, the United States would seek to exploit the weak theological justification for violence, in particular rationalizations for jihadist killing of innocents and Muslims and the use of suicide attacks.[23] To do this, the

---

[20] Means G. For a description of this means, see Daniel Byman, *Deadly Connections States that Sponsor Terrorism*, Cambridge, U.K.: Cambridge University Press, 2005.

[21] Means E.

[22] For RAND research describing the characteristics of this means, see James Bonomo, Giacomo Bergamo, David R. Frelinger, John Gordon, IV, and Brian A. Jackson, *Stealing the Sword: Limiting Terrorist Use of Advanced Conventional Weapons*, Santa Monica, Calif.: RAND Corporation, MG-510-DHS, 2007.

[23] Means J.

Table 3.6
Components of Counterterrorism Strategy 3

Components	Counterterrorism Strategy 3
Assessment of what al Qaeda needs to be able to inflict psychologically significant attacks in United States	Motivate leaders and recruits to undertake violent attacks
Overall strategy approach	Reduce influence of purveyors of jihadist ideas
Core priority means	Exploit weakened theological justification for violence; disrupt and capture motivational leaders; encourage defections from jihadist groups
Other possible priority means	Break up cooperation between al Qaeda and local jihadist groups (?)

United States would assist respected Islamic scholars and/or local reformers who are authoritative voices within their own societies. These individuals or groups would not necessarily be supportive of the United States but would be credible among their populations. U.S. assistance, primarily in the form of funding, would be aimed at media outlets, political parties, student and youth organizations, and labor unions. This assistance may need to be indirect and covert to protect the credibility of these individuals. The difficulty for the United States is that it is hard to find authoritative voices among Islamic theoreticians, and it is also unclear whether ideological arguments can divert potential recruits.[24]

Second, the United States would aim to capture and prosecute inspirational Salafi-jihadist leaders to degrade the ability of jihadist organizations to recruit and motivate their members.[25] These leaders may or may not be theological ideologues. The difficulty with this means is that the United States would need to convince governments to help locate, apprehend, and prosecute these motivational leaders.[26]

Third, the United States would take steps to encourage defections and facilitate individual separations from terrorist organizations as a way of undermining the legitimacy of these organizations among local populations and of reducing group membership.[27] Detainee populations in particular may be vulnerable to information about intra- and inter-group power struggles that raise the specter of group splintering, fracture, or dissolution and so make a preemptive exit more attractive. Appeals to members' material interests, such as the opportunity to work as a paid informant, financial support for family members, or amnesty may encourage exits from groups, while access to networks of other former members can ease reintroduction into society. It may also be possible to use periods of incarceration to inculcate an antiviolence ethic in detainees in the hope that they may then serve as credible sources for challenging the rheto-

---

[24] For RAND research describing the characteristics of this "means," see David Gompert *Heads We Win: Improving Cognitive Effectiveness in Counterinsurgency*, Santa Monica, Calif.: RAND Corporation, RB-9244-OSD, 2007; and Cragin and Gerwehr, 2005.

[25] Means K.

[26] For RAND research describing the characteristics of this means, see Angel Rabasa, Peter Chalk, Kim Cragin, Sara A. Daly, Heather S. Gregg, Theodore W. Karasik, Kevin A. O'Brien, and William Rosenau, *Beyond al-Qaeda: Part 1, The Global Jihadist Movement*, Santa Monica, Calif.: RAND Corporation, MG-429-AF, 2006a; Angel Rabasa, Peter Chalk, Kim Cragin, Sara A. Daly, Heather S. Gregg, Theodore W. Karasik, Kevin A. O'Brien, and William Rosenau, *Beyond al-Qaeda: Part 2, The Outer Rings of the Terrorist Universe*, Santa Monica, Calif.: RAND Corporation, MG-430-AF, 2006b; and Brian Michael Jenkins, *Unconquerable Nation: Knowing Our Enemy, Strengthening Ourselves*, Santa Monica, Calif.: RAND Corporation, MG-454-RC, 2006.

[27] Means M.

ric of motivational terrorist leaders. The scale of this means is limited, depending on access to detainees and voluntary defectors.[28]

Implementation. The State Department is pursuing a variety of public information programs that could be tailored to implement Strategy 3. Some of these are housed in the Bureau of Public Affairs, such as the Middle East Partnership Initiative, and others are in the Bureau of Democracy, Human Rights, and Humanitarian Assistance, including the Human Rights and Democracy Fund.[29] In addition, the State Department is clearly giving public information campaigns priority in its budget, having defined as a Strategic Goal for Peace and Security (Counterterrorism) the "number of public information campaigns completed by U.S. government programs." Their "indicator justification" is "winning the hearts and minds of local populations," and it defines these public information campaigns as including radio, public service announcements, print media, and Internet postings aimed at "de-legitimizing terrorist activities." Their target is 40 campaigns in FY 2009, up from the target of 29 in FY 2008.[30]

Challenges. The main challenge in Strategy 3 revolves around the difficulty Americans have in being credible in these types of activities. The United States risks the prospect of considerable backlash in the Muslim world when pursuing such activities, which, in turn, could aid jihadist propaganda. The United States will also face criticism from the international community for promoting policies that are inconsistent with its espoused support for religious freedom. Moreover, finding the purveyors of these ideas, and then either gaining their support or apprehending them, will not be easy.

Strategy 3: Other Possible Priority Means. Having defined the core priority means in Strategy 3, the next step is to decide whether to add as a priority a means that attempts to break up cooperation among violent jihadists through the use of public diplomacy and/or information operations.[31] The aim would be to alter local jihadists' perceptions of the contribution adopting al Qaeda's agenda and accepting support can make to their own pursuit of local political objectives. These activities would attempt to create or to deepen sources of religious or ethnic dissension and to widen ideological fault lines; this could be done either overtly or covertly.[32]

The argument in favor of giving priority in Strategy 3 to this means is that it could reduce the groups al Qaeda could count on to support them in their operations against the United States and also potentially the countries in which the al Qaeda core can operate. The argument against giving priority to this means is that the United States has very little leverage in influencing these local jihadists. To the extent that this means would involve U.S. cooperation

---

[28] For RAND research describing the characteristics of this means, see Jenkins, 2006; and Gregory Treverton and Heather S. Gregg, *Recruitment, Assimilation and Defection in Religious Movements: Board of Religious Experts,* workshop, Santa Monica, Calif.: RAND Corporation, 2007.

[29] U.S. Department of State, 2008, pp. 40–41, 503, 551–553.

[30] U.S. Department of State, 2008, p. 742.

[31] Means I.

[32] For RAND research describing the characteristics of this means, see Kim Cragin, Peter Chalk, Sara A. Daly, and Brian A. Jackson, *Sharing the Dragon's Teeth: Terrorist Groups and the Exchange of New Technologies,* Santa Monica, Calif.: RAND Corporation, MG-485-DHS, 2007; Rabasa et al., 2006a; Rabasa et al., 2006b; and William Rosenau, *Waging the "War of Ideas,"* reprinted from *McGraw-Hill Homeland Security Handbook,* October 10, 2005, Chapter 72, Santa Monica, Calif.: RAND Corporation, RP-1218, 2006.

with violent local jihadists, it could also undermine the central aims of Strategy 3: to support those in the Muslim community arguing against violence and to silence those promoting violent jihadist views.

Step 4: Facilitate Choice of a Strategy

The final step in our strategic planning approach is to set the stage for the choice of a strategy from among the defined alternatives, not to offer a recommendation.

Choosing Among the Counterterrorism Strategy Approaches

To be able to carry out psychologically significant attacks within the United States, al Qaeda would need many things, and these can be found in U.S. government strategy documents and the counterterrorism literature. What we have done in our strategic planning approach is to identify three alternative expert assessments of al Qaeda's *primary* requirement to be able to carry out psychologically significant attacks within the United States, and to use these assessments as the basis for defining three distinct counterterrorism strategies. The strategies give priority to different means, chosen in each case because they are viewed as being effective in denying jihadist groups the primary need identified by the given strategy.

The final step in our strategic planning approach is to find a systematic way to choose among the three strategies. Within the U.S. government, the decisionmaking process most often involves defining options and presenting the considerations in favor and against. So what considerations should inform the choice of one of these alternative counterterrorism strategies?

One consideration would be whether one of the assessments of what al Qaeda needs to carry out psychologically significant attacks in the United States is correct in its identification of the primary requirement. If so, the choice of that strategy would follow. For example, if to carry out attacks in the United States, al Qaeda *must* have a secure base, then "denying jihadists a safe haven" would be chosen as the strategy approach.

Selecting a strategy on this basis, however, is problematic, because an active global network (Strategy 1), a secure base (Strategy 2), and motivation for violent attacks (Strategy 3) would all be expected to be important to al Qaeda's ability to conduct an attack within the United States. It is difficult, in other words, to find a basis for determining that any one of these is truly the *primary* requirement. Nonetheless, one might judge that one of these, for example, "motivating leaders and recruits to undertake violent attacks," is relatively less important than the other two. In this case, the strategy approach of "reducing the influence of purveyors of jihadist ideas" would not be chosen.

Another consideration in evaluating the strategies would be how well the strategy approaches measure up with what is known about al Qaeda's history of operations and what has worked or not worked in terms of U.S. actions. For example, networks have been critical to al Qaeda's success in the past, but over the last seven years its leadership has proved resilient, able to reconstitute networks despite the counterterrorism efforts of the U.S. and its allies. So, disrupting jihadist activities (Strategy 1) may produce at best only very temporary effects on al Qaeda's ability to carry out attacks in the United States. Similarly, denying jihadists a safe haven (Strategy 2) in one place may be fairly easy, but keeping them from finding any place with ungoverned territory may be impossible. Ideas and ideology have also played a role in al

Qaeda recruiting (Strategy 3), but it is not clear that they have been the most important factor in motivating leaders or recruits. In sum, none of the strategies *promise* success, given what is known about what al Qaeda has done in the past.

Another consideration in evaluating the strategies would be whether al Qaeda currently has, or in the near future will have, capabilities that match the primary requirement identified in each strategy: For Strategy 1, this would be the presence of an active global network; for Strategy 2, this would be a secure base; and for Strategy 3, this would be a cadre of effective motivational leaders. One would ask, for example, whether al Qaeda could mount a psychologically significant attack within the United States given its current and near-term projected network of groups and individuals. If the answer is that this is unlikely, given the fragmentation of the jihadist groups and the core leadership's lack of effective tactical command and control, then the strategy approach of "disrupting violent jihadist groups' activities through counter-terrorism operations"—Strategy 1—would not be chosen.

Another consideration in evaluating the strategies would be to focus on the prospect of the United States being able to implement successfully the strategy approach. If, for example, the United States could not count on being able to create the political, economic, and security conditions necessary to deny jihadists safe havens, another strategy approach with a greater probability of success could be chosen. Selecting a strategy in this way, however, based not on what al Qaeda needs but on what the United States can do, may produce success in the implementation of the strategy's prioritized means but not necessarily achieve the strategic goal of preventing psychologically significant attacks from occurring within the United States.

From these considerations, one discovers many uncertainties, as is often the case in strategy choices facing government policymakers. This is clearly a primary reason why today the U.S. government has not defined a counterterrorism strategy in which the means are prioritized. Such uncertainties also provide a reason for doing more analysis prior to choosing a strategy, for example, focused on whether al Qaeda has the capabilities to match the primary requirement in each of the strategies. Or, as policymakers often do, one could choose based on some combination of these considerations and notwithstanding the uncertainties.

Steps to Take Once a Strategy Approach Is Chosen

Once a strategy approach is chosen, a number of steps would need to be undertaken to implement the strategy.

(1) Prioritization of Means and Countries. The countries to be the focus of the strategy will need to be selected, and decisions will need to be made about whether to give priority to the other possible means identified for the chosen strategy. Whether and how other non-priority means might be employed to support and reinforce the priority means will also need to be considered. The means would then need to be fleshed out in detail in terms of the specific tasks necessary to accomplish them.

(2) Implementation. Decisions will be needed about which government and private programs will be used to implement the means, and about the funds that are to be committed. For strategies with a specific focus on individual countries, it will be necessary to allocate resources in a way so that those countries receive priority funding within the State, Treasury, and Defense Department budgets.

(3) Coordination. Policymakers will need to address how to implement the counterterrorism strategy in the context of other U.S. national security policies, given that there likely will be opportunities for linkages, as well as tensions, in terms of where and how to apply U.S.

political capital and other resources. One example of an opportunity for linkage would be the possibility of connecting the priority means chosen in a counterterrorism strategy to efforts to prevent terrorists from acquiring WMD. In terms of tensions, it will be difficult in the near future to implement the military assistance requirements if Strategy 1 is chosen, given current commitments of the military training assets in Iraq and Afghanistan. Moreover, shifts in resources away from any country in a State Department or DoD program will always be resisted because of concerns about the need for ongoing support from that country on other potential issues of importance.

(4) Documentation. Strategy and policy documents will need to be written. In some cases, these will be made public, and in others they will provide classified internal guidance. With a clearly defined counterterrorism strategy, it would be possible not only to define priorities but also to provide specific guidance for the allocation of resources, for example in the DoD *Guidance for Development of the Force* and *Guidance for Employment of the Force.*

We can anticipate that the nature of the jihadist threat will change over time and in response to the implementation of a chosen counterterrorism strategy. As such, it will be necessary to review regularly the priorities within the chosen strategy, and even the strategy itself. In some cases, a reprioritization of means may be needed; in others, a transition from one strategy to another—for example, if Strategy 1 is implemented and succeeds in seriously disrupting the al Qaeda network, it would be logical then to consider adopting either Strategy 2 or 3.

CHAPTER FOUR

Implementing the Strategic Planning Approach Within the U.S. Government

This report has described *an* approach to strategic planning, the process of identifying strategic goals and the prioritizing of means to achieve them, in order to provide policymakers within the U.S. government with a way of undertaking strategic planning. We have illustrated how one might implement the four-step approach using the example of defining counterterrorism strategies. In addition to the alternative strategies that emerged, this exercise uncovered insights into how to organize thinking about the issues that arise in pursuing a counterterrorism strategy and how resources in current government programs might be focused. Again, we undertook this exercise for purely illustrative purposes: We are not advocating any specific roadmap, operational plan, or bureaucratic solution to the counterterrorism challenges discussed here.

We also discovered that in this case, even in a research environment, it is not easy to set priorities or to choose among the strategies, given the many uncertainties associated with al Qaeda capabilities and the potential effectiveness of U.S. counterterrorism policies.

Uncertainties in today's world are among the reasons that the current process for strategic planning for national security within the U.S. government does not involve the setting of priorities. There are also political and bureaucratic reasons. But planning using the approach presented here could not only improve the effectiveness of policies but also help in the allocation of limited resources when pressures to cut government budgets are increasing. How might our strategic planning approach be implemented within the U.S. government national security policymaking process?

Deciding on the national security policies amenable to strategic planning and their scope would be the first task. Those that involve military operations (Iraq or Afghanistan) or intense diplomatic negotiations (North Korea's nuclear programs) would not be good candidates, as the policies need to be defined daily and involve primarily tactical and not strategic choices. Such policies could, however, be candidates for strategic planning in advance of undertaking operations or negotiations. Other policies, especially those that call for the application of both political and military means, would be good candidates, and then the choice should depend on the criticality of the policy to overall U.S. national security interests. This list of critical policies could then be narrowed using different criteria, e.g., those where conflict exists or could arise (the Middle East peace process; China/Taiwan policy); those requiring presidential involvement (WMD proliferation); those where a consensus is lacking within the bureaucracy, etc.

In real-world policymaking, the intellectual steps in our strategic planning approach would need to be undertaken in a very different environment from that at RAND: one where officials from many departments and agencies bring expertise as well as strong bureaucratic interests, where decision-making responsibility is highly decentralized, and where resistance exists not only to making choices but also to any changes in existing policies. Even the gathering of intelligence and information, which is critical to each of the steps in the strategic planning approach, comes from organizations with competing bureaucratic perspectives.

Implementing our strategic planning approach inside the U.S. government will, therefore, require a top-down decisionmaking process, orchestrated by the Assistant to the President for National Security Affairs, on behalf of the President, and with the personal engagement of the department secretaries and agency heads and a few trusted staff. The information and analyses needed to implement the steps in the approach would be gathered from across the government, but choices would need to be made in private by the President and National Security Council (NSC) principals. Critical to being able to consider new directions and changes in current policies will be preventing media leaks.

The choice of a strategy would be informed by a background paper that would flesh out each of the steps in our strategic planning approach for the chosen national security topic. The first step is to define and operationalize the strategic goal; a single "straw man" formulation would be presented, along with a supporting rationale.

The second step, to define the means to achieve the strategic goal, should involve not only means being pursued as policies today but also those that are new, and therefore would potentially require a choice between old and new. Each of the means needs to be defined in detail as to what policies and programs would be involved, along with what is currently being done and planned, and also how effective each of the means has been in the past. The third step is defining alternative strategies; these need to be analytically derived, based on assessments of the factors that might threaten achievement of the strategic goal. The alternatives should not be bureaucratically driven, i.e., one diplomatic alternative and one military alternative, and they need to be substantive, not, as is often the case in the government, "straw men" that cannot compete with the single bureaucratic consensus. Pros and cons would then be developed for each of the alternatives, along with a description of the most important considerations that should inform the choice of a strategy.

If consensus can be reached on a strategy through NSC discussions, the Assistant to the President for National Security Affairs would then work with the NSC principals in finalizing a decision document that lays out the strategy (explaining how the means would be prioritized and integrated in a way to achieve the strategic goal) in enough detail to guide the operations and budgets of the involved government departments and agencies. They would also assemble a strategy document outlining the priorities and rationale for presentation to Congress and the American public. The normal NSC, Office of Management and Budget, and department processes would provide the means to ensure that the goals and priorities in the strategy are carried out in day-to-day policies and budgets.

In the end, even if a single strategy with prioritized means is not chosen, going through the steps in our strategic planning approach has advantages. It can help clarify what one aims to achieve for the specific national security policy topic, uncover underlying assumptions, and illuminate the critical and contentious issues. Most importantly, it would mean a decision to pursue all means without any prioritization was undertaken not by default but, rather, consciously, because it was identified as being the best available course of action.

Bibliography

RAND Research Used in the Counterterrorism Illustration

Bonomo, James, Giacomo Bergamo, David R. Frelinger, John Gordon, IV, and Brian A. Jackson, *Stealing the Sword: Limiting Terrorist Use of Advanced Conventional Weapons*, Santa Monica, Calif.: RAND Corporation, MG-510-DHS, 2007. As of December 10, 2008:
http://www.rand.org/pubs/monographs/MG510/

Byman, Daniel, *Deadly Connections States that Sponsor Terrorism*, Cambridge, U.K.: Cambridge University Press, 2005.

Cragin, Kim, and Scott Gerwehr, *Disuading Terror: Strategic Influence and the Struggle Against Terrorism*, Santa Monica, Calif.: RAND Corporation, MG-184-RC, 2005. As of December 10, 2008:
http://www.rand.org/pubs/monographs/MG184/

Cragin, Kim, Peter Chalk, Sara A. Daly, and Brian A. Jackson, *Sharing the Dragon's Teeth: Terrorist Groups and the Exchange of New Technologies*, Santa Monica, Calif.: RAND Corporation, MG-485-DHS, 2007. As of December 10, 2008:
http://www.rand.org/pubs/monographs/MG485/

Davis, Paul K. and Brian Michael Jenkins. *Deterrence and Influence in Counterterrorism: A Component in the War on al Qaeda*. Santa Monica, Calif.: RAND Corporation, MR-1619-DARPA 2002. As of December 10, 2008:
http://www.rand.org/pubs/monograph_reports/MR1619/

Don, Bruce W., Dave Frelinger, Scott Gerwehr, Eric Landree, Brian A. Jackson, *RAND Network Technologies for Networked Terrorists: Assessing the Value of Information and Communications Technologies to Modern Terrorist Organizations*, Santa Monica, Calif.: RAND Corporation, TR-454-DHS, 2007. As of December 10, 2008:
http://www.rand.org/pubs/technical_reports/TR454/

Gompert, David C., *Heads We Win: Improving Cognitive Effectiveness in Counterinsurgency*, Santa Monica, Calif.: RAND Corporation, RB-9244-OSD, 2007. As of December 10, 2008:
http://www.rand.org/pubs/research_briefs/RB9244/

Gompert, David C., John Gordon, IV, Adam Grissom, David R. Frelinger, Seth G. Jones, Martin C. Libicki, Edward O'Connell, Brooke K. Stearns, and Robert E. Hunter, *War by Other Means: Building Complete and Balanced Capabilities for Counterinsurgency*, Santa Monica, Calif.: RAND Corporation, MG-595/2-OSD, 2008. As of December 10, 2008:
http://www.rand.org/pubs/monographs/MG595.2/

Grissom, Adam, and David Ochmanek, *Train, Equip, Advise, Assist: The USAF and the Indirect Approach to Countering Terrorist Groups Abroad*, Santa Monica, Calif.: RAND Corporation, MG-699-AF, 2008, not available to the general public.

Haims, Marla C., David C. Gompert, Gregory F. Treverton, and Brooke K. Stearns, *Breaking the Failed-State Cycle*, Santa Monica, Calif.: RAND Corporation, OP-204-HLTH/NDRI/A/AF, 2008. As of December 10, 2008:
http://www.rand.org/pubs/occasional_papers/OP204/

Hoffman, Bruce. *Inside Terrorism*, revised and expanded edition, New York: Columbia University Press, 2006.

Hoffman, Bruce. *The Use of the Internet by Islamic Extremists.* Testimony presented to House Permanent Select Committee on Intelligence, May 4, 2006. As of December 10, 2008:
http://www.rand.org/pubs/testimonies/CT262-1/

Hoffman, Bruce, and Kim Cragin. "Four Lessons from Five Countries." *RAND Review,* Vol. 26, No. 2 (2002), 42–43. As of December 10, 2008:
http://www.rand.org/publications/randreview/issues/rr.08.02/fourlessons.html

Hosmer, Stephen T., *Operations Against Enemy Leaders*, Santa Monica, Calif.: RAND Corporation, MR-1385-AF, 2001. As of December 10, 2008:
http://www.rand.org/pubs/monograph_reports/MR1385

Jenkins, Brian Michael, *Unconquerable Nation: Knowing Our Enemy, Strengthening Ourselves*, Santa Monica, Calif.: RAND Corporation, MG-454-RC, 2006. As of December 10, 2008:
http://www.rand.org/pubs/monographs/MG454/

Jones, Seth G., and Martin Libicki, *How Terrorist Groups End: Lessons for Countering al Qa'ida*, Santa Monica, Calif.: RAND Corporation, MG-741/1-RC, 2008. As of December 10, 2008:
http://www.rand.org/pubs/monographs/MG741/

Jones, Seth G., Jeremy M. Wilson, Andrew Rathmell, and K. Jack Riley, *Establishing Law and Order After Conflict*, Santa Monica, Calif.: RAND Corporation, MG-374-RC, 2005. As of December 10, 2008:
http://www.rand.org/pubs/monographs/MG374/

Libicki, Martin C., David C. Gompert, David R. Frelinger, and Raymond Smith, *Byting Back: Regaining Information Superiority Against 21st Century Insurgents*, Santa Monica, Calif: RAND Corporation, MG-595/1-OSD. As of December 10, 2008:
http://www.rand.org/pubs/monographs/MG595.1/

Moroney, Jennifer D.P., Nancy E. Blacker, Renee Buhr, James McFadden, Cathryn Quantic Thurston, and Anny Wong, *Building Partner Capabilities for Coalition Operations*, Santa Monica, Calif.: RAND Corporation, MG-635-A, 2007. As of December 10, 2008:
http://www.rand.org/pubs/monographs/MG635/

Ochmanek, David, *Military Operations Against Terrorist Groups Abroad: Implications for the United States Air Force*, Santa Monica, Calif.: RAND Corporation, MR-1738-AF, 2003. As of December 10, 2008:
http://www.rand.org/pubs/monograph_reports/MR1738

Rabasa, Angel, Peter Chalk, Kim Cragin, Sara A. Daly, Heather S. Gregg, Theodore W. Karasik, Kevin A. O'Brien, and William Rosenau, *Beyond al-Qaeda: Part 1, The Global Jihadist Movement*, Santa Monica, Calif.: RAND Corporation, MG-429-AF, 2006a. As of December 10, 2008:
http://www.rand.org/pubs/monographs/MG429/

Rabasa, Angel, Peter Chalk, Kim Cragin, Sara A. Daly, Heather S. Gregg, Theodore W. Karasik, Kevin A. O'Brien, and William Rosenau, *Beyond al-Qaeda: Part 2, The Outer Rings of the Terrorist Universe*, Santa Monica, Calif.: RAND Corporation, MG-430-AF, 2006b. As of December 10, 2008:
http://www.rand.org/pubs/monographs/MG430/

Rabasa, Angel, Steven Boraz, Peter Chalk, Kim Cragin, Theodore W. Karasik, Jennifer D. P. Moroney, Kevin A. O'Brien, and John E. Peters, *Ungoverned Territories: Understanding and Reducing Terrorism Risks*, Santa Monica, Calif.: RAND Corporation, MG-561-AF, 2007. As of December 10, 2008:
http://www.rand.org/pubs/monographs/MG561/

Rosenau, William, *Waging the "War of Ideas,"* reprinted from *McGraw-Hill Homeland Security Handbook*, October 10, 2005, Chapter 72, Santa Monica, Calif.: RAND Corporation, RP-1218, 2006. As of December 10, 2008:
http://www.rand.org/pubs/reprints/RP1218/

Treverton, Gregory and Heather S. Gregg, *Recruitment, Assimilation and Defection in Religious Movements: Board of Religious Experts,* workshop, Santa Monica, Calif: RAND Corporation, 2007.

Other References

Aspin, Les, Secretary of Defense, *Report on the BOTTOM_UP REVIEW*, October 1993.

Bovey Robert L., and James S. Thomason, *National Security Memorandum 3 (NSSM-3): A Pivotal Initiative in U.S. Defense Policy Development,* Institute for Defense Analyses, September 1998.

Joint Chiefs of Staff, *National Military Strategy of the United States of America*, 2004

Kennan, George F. (writing as 'X'), "The Sources of Soviet Conduct," *Foreign Affairs*, Vol. 25, No. 4, July 1947, pp. 566–582, reprinted in *American Diplomacy 1900–1950*, Chicago: University of Chicago Press, 1951, p. 113.

National Security Council, *NSC-68: United States Objectives and Programs for National Security*, April 14, 1950.

———, "National Security Memorandum 246: National Defense Policy and Military Posture," September 2, 1976. As of December 10, 2008:
http://www.ford.utexas.edu/LIBRARY/document/nsdmnssm/nssm246a.htm

Nottberg, Tyler, "Once and Future Policy Planning: Solarium for Today," Web page, The Eisenhower Institute, undated. As of December 10, 2008:
http://www.eisenhowerinstitute.org/about/living_history/solarium_for_today.dot

U.S. Department of Defense, Defense Security Cooperation Agency, *Fiscal Year (FY) 2009 Budget Estimates*, February 2008.

———, *National Defense Strategy*, June 2008.

U.S. Department of State, *Congressional Budget Justification, Foreign Operations, Fiscal Year 2009*, February 19, 2008.

The White House, "Comprehensive Net Assessment and Military Force Posture Review," Presidential Review Memorandum/NSC-10, February 18, 1977.

———, *National Security Strategy of the United States of America*, September 2002.

———, *National Security Strategy of the United States of America*, March 2006.

———, *National Strategy for Combating Terrorism*, September 2006.